MW01274826

Talking
With
Trees

William Ratcliffe

ISBN-10:0692684026
ISBN-13: 978-0692684023

Talking With Trees

To Listen to Trees
is pretty easy
-you just have to be
very Very Quiet
Gratitude—to the trees who talk:
Helen's Ancient Yew at Schumacher
Esther at OSA
The Back Yard Cedar
Clan at the top of the Pass
And Countless others who have taken the time to let
me listen to their wisdom
BiL 2016

" gonna convince ur mirror
like yve never done before
before givin substance to mirror
givin substance ever more

& you assure you've got
something to offer
Something shiny & new
but how much of you
is repetition
what u did wi per 2hoz

I see ur self pity shining
cos the tears roll down
ur cheek

CONTENTS

1 PRECIPICE(PRELUDE)

Like a Tree on a Precipice

Roots grip silently

To life

Water seeps

Frost cracks

Roots expand

Rock erodes.

Repeat.

Each day a bonus before gravity wins

Time stands still for no Tree.

2 TREE (INVOCATION)

The liquid of our dreams, the liquid of our psyche, the

liquid of our divine,

Swirling in the molecules that become ourselves

You humans, You think you are gods---brothers—and

sisters and children of gods.

A tree dies in the forest ---What does it sound like?

The death of a tree.

I hear one screaming now.

Man, You man- yes, you…

What does it feel like to kill a tree.

As the shovel moves thru the living green forest does the

tree feel anxious, fear, Dread?

What does the tree feel when the blade rips her roots from

the ground?

3

When the blade tears into her bark and rips into her veins.

When the blade shreds her fibers and guts her core.

You humans and your metal monsters.

What does the tree feel?

The tree screams.

She screams in decibels you cannot hear,

in languages you have no clue about

She screams in dimensions beyond your comprehension.

She screams for our brothers and sisters who are extinct.

That is what a tree feels when she dies.

She will not exhale life giving oxygen

She will not stand in the sun,

Pull water from the earth,

Create fruit for humans.

She will sigh a final sigh

spill her seeds and sap onto the earth

A creature of the divine-

Dead

3 HEART OF A TREE

The beat of the vortex.

The beat of a portal.

The vortex of conscious that is every being.

The portal of love that is every thing

.

I asked a Tree

What does the heart of a tree look like

Heart of a Tree

Thump thump

Thummmp thuummmp.

Thuuummmmmmmmp. Thhhuuuummmmmmmmmmp.

7

A tree told me

in a heart to heart talk

Our Hearts beat as One

In a time, space, walk

Heart beat flows up

Heart beat flows down.

Heart Beat connects

every sacred clown

My out to Your in

Our vortexes dance

My in to Your out

Our portals prance

We dance with the breath of Gaia

Under tears of rain

With the warm heart of love

We heal Our pain

My heart beats slow

Your heart beats fast

But together they beat

To the next last.

Ohmmmmmmmm

The heart of a tree looks like your heart,

looks like my heart.

The heart of a tree looks like love.

Ohmmmmmmm

BiL 2015(with thanks to a few wizards)

4 HOW TO BURN A WEDDING ALBUM

Get married—have an amazing set of sisters who create a wedding album

A few years later get a divorce.

Box up album

Write on it don't open for 10 years.

Wait ten years.

Open box—find bits and pieces from the wedded life--- and a book of amazing pictures.

Go thru album-—saving enough to keep the memories alive---the picture of the uncle who passed, the friends we don't speak to any more, the flower girls, the best friend who committed suicide.

And one or two of the bride and groom with tears of joy in their eyes.

Start a fire with deep intention---realize this is a sacred fire to give the moment to the ages and commit a time and space to the Past.

Open up album—think of the moments when love was the power of connection. The kisses, the adventures, the partner embrace.

Put the first page on the fire.

The hearts that say "I love you " and "forever and always"

Watch the pictures curl in the flame.

Think of the shared songs- Shared dances.

Think of the apathy, the tears, the immature emotional moments.

Add another page to the flame

Think of the chaos, think of the betrayals, the broken trust.

Think of lonely nights, of anger, of jealousy.

Watch as the picture bubbles, the faces distort, and

become ash,

Moments of self-hatred reflected back by your partner.

Add a page.

Think of the first kiss, Think of her eyes, her smile

Think of how much you loved her when you stared into her eyes and asked "Will you marry me?"

Add a page.

Think of the shared tears, the hand holding in crisis, the sobbing muffled by hugs.

Add a page.

Think of the words-"I want a divorce".

add a page.

As I stare into the ashes, I realize we are just momentary beings of light here on this plane.

I am a child of the divine. She is a child of the divine.

We are, and were, children of the divine.

My heart fills with sorrow at my actions and reactions.

At my contribution to these ashes.

Thank you for loving me during a time I struggled to love

myself.

Thank you for saying "Yes." those many years ago

My heart fills with gratitude for the time we spent, good
and bad.

And I find the space to Forgive Us.

And Myself.

Tears fall down my face.

I taste them

And I let them go.

I dance in release.

OOOOHHHHMMMM

2014 BiL

5 THE FAIRY AND THE FENIX
(FLOODLAND)

Break on thru

Sometimes you have to burn your art to really love it

Magical Fairy Dust

I stop the pain I do not feel

The shrouded sun hides behind a distant peak

as she rides the blood red smoke from the tears of trees

and the burnt dreams of humans

on her daily pilgrimage.

The light of night slowly rises,

The celestial dance begins.

I am on a windy dusty promontory, alone by choice.

I have spread my pain, my anger, and it hurts,

hurts those who love me

Trust me.

Want me.

I reach deep inside the divine that is me and ask for it to

stop,

I cannot do this anymore.

The cliff below me beckons

Come fly with me-whispers the wind.

My toes touch the edge

When you fill your (h)art with self-burning

it only shows how temporary we all are

I dance in the chill wind my crow feathers fluttering.

Oh radiant sun touch my heart

Oh wise owl fly with me

Oh warriors light guide me

A unicorn tear drop touches me.

I float I dive I swoop

Wind loud in my being

Strong the breath of Gaia supports me

As I dance on this worn rock.

Swhoosh

Whooshhh

No ego no super ego no id,

Just a human alone under the stars.

A thorn stabs my feet

Ouch

A little of my mortal soul on the dry dust

The blood price of really good art.

A rainbow warrior's tear touches my psyche

shatters me

fractal parts

broken jagged bits

green shard(jealousy)

red shard(angry passion)

purple shard

blue sadness shard

yellow fear shard.

flaying me alive

The beat begins

And I dance with my fractal self

My self who loves,

Myself who hates,

Myself who mourns,

My artist self, my animal self, my omnificent self,

Warrior self, present self, magic self

Love hate fear

I explode a flaming plasma of self-hatred

ARGHHHHHH!!!!!!

Ashes of self-destruction

Into Collapse

Compressed exhausted I am ASH

Just stop

Just stop

Just Stop.

A cosmological magic lover's tear touches me across time

and space

My fractal love

Resplendent in her plumage of shimmering amazing

rainbows

The lover who broke me

The lover I broke

The lover who broke her heart on my heart

The angel the mermaid, the warrior, the mother goddess,

the artist, The Fairy.

The beat continues

I hold out my hand inviting touch

My fractal lovers move with me.

Beat of the universe

We spin and become one

Ohm my soul resonates ohm ohm   ohmm

I am the beat of the universe

My lover fairy whispers in my ear

"All I can do is reflect love ohmmm" -((or)of my own self

I can do nothing))

I hug myself and dance

My legs are my legs

My arms are my arms

My head is my head.

I am dancing with the cosmic stars

Tears of love touch me.

A vibrant flow in my 3rd eye beams ecstasy to the universe

Ohm

The fading desert night grabs me. Thru the rising radiance

I am aware of deeper patterns of perfection.

From my cliff I see the waves of time eroding the hills and

valleys

We are all fluid you and I

The dawn sun blood fluorescent red

Ancient energy lines appear to me

Flashes of falling starlight in the sky

Ohm

Love Is the best armor, the best sword

I can choose my energy…

I Chose Love

A lonely tear touches me

I need humans.

Break the vial this journey is done

Balance begins to return.

As I come back a human fairy greets me, hugs me, feels

me

Our souls touch

We are human.

"How was your night?"

Ohmmm is all I can reply

as a tear of gratitude drips down my cheek.

and I taste life.

BiL 2015

6 ARBIET MACHT FRIE
("the work will make you free"—sign over the entrance
to the Auschwitz Death Camp)

Disintegration of the social fabric

This morning I woke up with the phrase "arbiet macht Frie". I was dreaming of concentration camps and death. --- my companion commented on it—something about 1940's—I replied Andrews Sisters and the draft—my friend got all holy and explained what the phrase meant—Auschwitz, death, Jews, ovens. However I was already 10 steps ahead….. and I really didn't want to spend the day explaining it.

What I really wanted to reply was "Arbiet Macht Frie" is the name of my new temp agency and bar-b-que joint—but that might be a little tasteless.

Watch out for the ghost train in the tunnel. It was humans who loaded the trains. It was humans driving the trains. It was humans on the trains

Tchhh thchhh thchhhhh

The beat of the tunnel

tChoo tchoo tchoo

I was just following orders

Whoo whooo

We cannot hide from our own ignorance.

Cogs in corporate wheels....

slotted in commuters....

wage slave consumers

The insides of the brains are talking and I am not listening.

Clackity Clack

We are loading boxcars with the souls of extinct beings to
feed

The all-consuming crematorium that illuminates how
much we hate our disconnected selves.

When this is how we treat our human brothers,

our brother trees don't stand a chance.

Crying eyes of the children of Afghanistan

begging for their stories to be told.

Dance you greedy motherfuckers dance

We are fucking ourselves.   And we know it.   So we do
everything in our power to not feel the pain.

Ouch motherfuckers ouch.

BiL 2011

7 COME DANCE WITH ME
(INSPIRED BY C. RAE)

Take my hand

Come dance with me

Under the goddess tree

Come dance with me in the meadow

Come dance with me all day

Come dance with me in the forest

Come dance with me I pray

Come dance with me in thistle

Come dance with me and swing

Come dance with me in flowers

Come dance along the spring

Come dance with me with bass

Come dance with me with sass

Come dance with me on a bicycle

As we fly across the grass

Come dance with me tomorrow

Come dance with me tonight

Come dance with me for Gaia

Come dance with me for light

Come dance with me in sorrow

Come dance with me for tears

Come dance with me for dying

Come dance away our fears

Come dance with me by fire

Come dance with me at night

Come dance with me in the dark

after Shadows fight

Come dance with me in joy

Come dance with me in rain

Come dance with me barefoot

Come dance with me in pain

Come dance for those who can

Come dance for those who can't

Come dance for those who will

Come dance for those who won't

Come dance with me at sunset

Come dance with me in flight

Come dance with my dark shadows

Dispelled by rae of light.

Come dance with me in the meadow

Come dance with me in grace

for all that is divine

on earth and sea and space

dance for moon

dance for sun

dance for stars

dance for love

dance for joy

dance dance dance

dance in this moment

dance in this life

dance is my soul

dance is my life

Take my hand

Come dance with me

under the goddess tree

OHMMMMMM

BiL 2014

8 THE TWO TREES

I stand between two trees

One a Cedar, the other a Spruce.

Tree souls together

root hairs touch

Sharing energy

Sharing nutrients

Sharing life

My arms touch each bark

Energy arcs

Thru my heart

Thru my pelvis

Thru my soul to the mycelium grounding under my

feet.

I am an energy bridge and we Amplify

A broadcast of love to the stars

Chaos and harmony

Exploding light!!!!

(breathe)

Ever fall in love with a tree?

Resonate as lovers?

Have you laughed with trees as branches dance in the

wind?

without trees there is no life -Lungs of the earth

Imagine a world without trees.

Just Be together,

All we have to do is

Just Be.

Harmony

Until Gaia's gravity wins in a storm.

Left untouched,

Long after our monkey foot prints fade,

My friends will sway

Branches touching

Under the sun, moon and stars

Sentinels to the connecting energy of brotherhood

They release me.

Our conversation over

Our moment done.

Gratitude.

BiL 2014

9 FLOWERS ON A BLUFF
(For the Angel, the Dragon,
The Mermaid, and the Witch)

Flowers on a bluff over a rocky beach

A bloom of me

A bloom of you

A bloom of lovers past, lovers present, lovers future

Each petal a vortex (Stamen)

Each leaf a vibration (Pistil)

Each flower a connecting wave, a simple soul, a tone

The breath of Gaia blows

And we dance

And our wave fronts collide.

Harmonies emerge

Dissonance erupts

Passions Roar

Crescendo

Diminuendo

Crescendo

Perdendo

Crescendo

Morendo

Sotto voce.

A moment of crest

A moment of trough

A moment of still

Our patterns of interference merge

Mosaics of dancing highs

Dancing lows

Of dancing silence

This simple symphonic dance between our hearts

Our souls and our desires

Ohmmmmmmm

BiL 2015

10 WING'ED MERMAID

Exhausted I walk despondent thru a dark dank

forest world.

The damp mist chills the soul of my spine.

I chance upon a spring flowing from a mossy tree.

I am thirsty, but I do not trust the water.

A rae of light bursts thru the treetops and,

I see a shimmering velvet wildflower.

The flower smiles.

I look closer.

This not flower is alive,

With shiny bright eyes

Silver flashing tail, shimmering rainbow wings

She hovers around me.

I feel a laugh in my head.

"Are you real?"

The laugh gains confidence and fills my soul.

She lands on my shoulder and I hear our souls

converse.

"do you trust me?"

I breathe

"Do you trust me?

A shiver of hope and gratitude, courses thru my body.

"If you trust me drink of the spring."

I touch the flowing cool water. I put my wet finger tips

in my mouth.

And I taste.

My mouth fills with water- the quenching water flows

across my lips, down my throat, deep into my stomach.

I gulp the flowing water down with gusto.

Bright Intense Loving Energy Fills My Mind

My lips touch other lips, an intense full mouth kiss

tongues touching pressing probing,

Lips Rubbing, Licking, Engulfing.

I am kissing the wing'ed mermaid.

Transformed we touch hands and dance to the rhythm

of the spring, the trees, the rain, the beam of sunlight.

The forest a cathedral for this moment.

We spin -her wings beating faster and faster beyond

space beyond time beyond ourselves.

My body fills with the lightness of loving soul

I breathe.

My eyes open .

A laughing wing'ed mermaid lands on my shoulder and

whispers "welcome to my world".

Ha haaa haaaaaa

Trees shake with my joyful laugh.

I am not alone.

BiL 2014 (the green man)

11 SHAKESPEARE'S GLOBE

The Remains of Shakespeare's Globe are here in this space

Campfire becomes sacred

In spaces deep

Within our DNA

We create sacred place

With ritual dance

Sacred becomes temple

Mythic stories

Of our dream world

From divine songs

Dear to our hearts

Temple becomes stage

Soulful reflections

Of our psyche

Hidden by Masks

Of our divinities

Stage becomes spectacle

Our heroic tales

Fill the arena

Gather dark dreams

Worship the flame

Spectacle becomes fire

Up and down

The helical spiral stairway

To our animal past

And our ethereal future.

Fire becomes embers

Ashes of civilizations

Erode until

The spark of sacred

Ignites Paleolithic campfire

Embers become ruins

Ruins become sacred

Until the land is eroded into the seas.

And then the Dolphins will find sacred space to swim.

And they will call it Theater—

The Remains of Shakespeare's Globe are here in this

Place

BiL 2011

12 TRAGEDY

The real tragedy it that it is preventable.

Real tragedy is that we have thought about it.

Tragedy that our civilization is gonna crash and die.

The real tragedy is that I will die.

Real tragedy is that you will die.

Tragedy that our ancestors did die.

The real tragedy is that my last relationship died.

Real tragedy is that we have to suffer loss.

Tragedy that almost every human being that has ever lived on this planet who was born before 1900 is dead.

We rarely live a century.

The real hope is we are all part of a continuum and get to go back down the rabbit hole a couple of more times.

BiL 2011

13 THE SMALLEST INFINITE RING (POSTLUDE)

The smallest infinite ring-(small bell chime)

Our birth as a place to see and be and dance

As we all go down together ---as we sink into the abyss---

as the human earth floats through the ether to the end of

time. What will the last humans think?

As we all go down together ---as we sink into the abyss---

as the human less earth floats through the ether to the end

of time. What will humans think---will they know they are

dead?

As we go down together -as we sink into the abyss---as the

earth floats to the end of time what will their temples look

like.

As we all go down into the abyss--- the earth floats

through the ether. Who will play in the eroded temples.

the abyss the earth floats the last temples the last humans

Is the Earth just a playground for our Eternal Souls?

Oh dear Love and all that is Divine

Come into my heart

Help us Save ourselves, save our planet

Help us Love ourselves, love our planet

We are worth saving.

I am in the heart of the universe.

if we fail as stewards mother earth will just chose another.

Peace be with you.

Thank you gentle folk.

OHHHMMMMMMMMMMMMMM

The last syllable of recorded time

O

H

M

M

m

m

m

MY NOTES

My Friend Helen asked me if I had ever felt the energy of a Tree. I said "no". She led me to Ancient Yew in an old church yard and I felt the life of the tree resonate with me. A classic deep ecology moment. When we were done I asked the tree---"how can I help tell your story." That was a lifetime ago.

Two years ago my Gaia Tree Project (a surreal radio drama) was stuck, I was stuck. I met Esther—the magical mother tree tended by my fairy friend Danielle at Our Sacred Acres. My conversation with Esther went something like—"Howdy Tree, I am trying to tell your story and I need some help with healing in order to finish this one. Ohmmm. " The next year was a very intense healing vision quest—every time I was stuck I talked to Esther and I would find myself on another quest. Each quest challenged my deeply held structures of reality—and shattered them. It took me a year to put the pieces of my soul back together.

Tree oriented healing came to me when I needed it most---thank you Dee and the trees of Breitenbush.

The Cedar Out of Place—she embraces me every time I have needed to feel the energy of a tree—and she has taught me how to celebrate trees---they like prayer flags. Heart with Wings, your encouragement during the final process has been magical. I can only Reflect.

Each work in this volume has a story—some were written for a project called *The Gaia Tree(or why does humanity insist on committing geno-suicide)*, others were written after particularly grueling pilgrimages or personal interactions. And some were written to find hope---to lose hope is to lose love and to dance with the sacred clowns is the best way I know to regain hope. The divine is laughing because She has been there(and She is Us). Humanities best hope is radical optimism. Choose it. With gratitude to all that is Divine. OHmmmmmm

BiL—2016